UNDER THE
MICROSCOPE
EARTH'S TINIEST INHABITANTS

Life Books for Kids | Children's Science & Nature Books

GW00578202

BABY PROFESSOR BOOKS

First Edition, 2019

Published in the United States by Speedy Publishing LLC, 40 E Main Street, Newark, Delaware 19711 USA.

© 2019 Baby Professor Books, an imprint of Speedy Publishing LLC

Baby Professor Books are available at special discounts when purchased in bulk for industrial and sales-promotional use. For details contact our Special Sales Team at Speedy Publishing LLC, 40 E Main Street, Newark, Delaware 19711 USA. Telephone (888) 248-4521 Fax: (210) 519-4043. www.speedybookstore.com

10 9 8 7 6 * 5 4 3 2 1

Print Edition: 9781541968684

Digital Edition: 9781541968745

Hardcover Edition: 9781541968714

See the world in pictures. Build your knowledge in style.
https://www.speedypublishing.com/

CONTENTS

There's a whole new world somewhere in Earth, somewhere you can't easily see. The reason is because this whole new world is made up for tiny organisms that are difficult to see with the naked eyes. Because they're so tiny, these organisms are not easily avoidable and may even wreck havoc in the body's internal processes if they get in.

In this book, we're going to read about some of Earth's tiniest inhabitants and how they interact with all other forms of life. Let's get started.

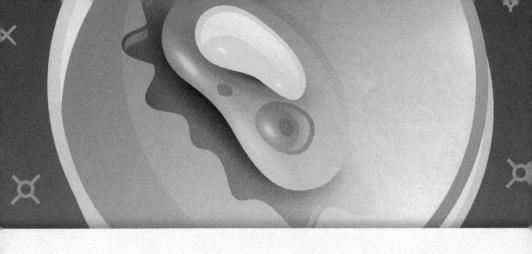

CHAPTER 1
What are Bacteria?

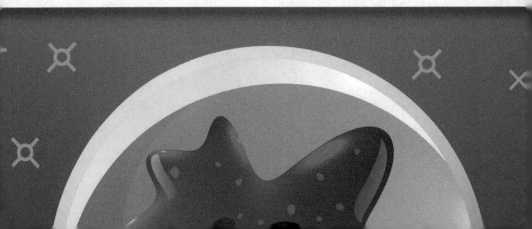

Bacteria are very simple prokaryotic microorganisms. Prokaryotic simply means that their cell structure is very basic.

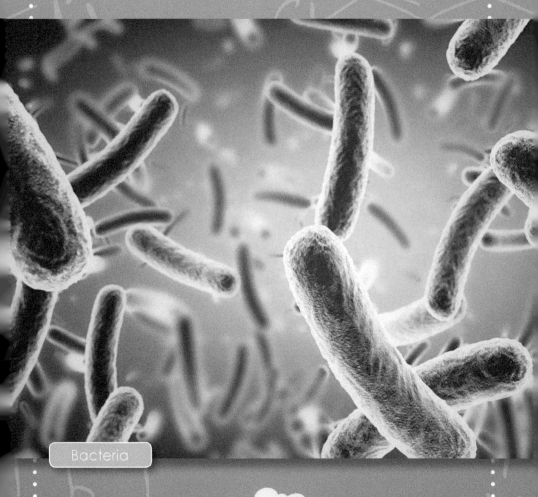

Bacteria

Bacteria Cell Anatomy

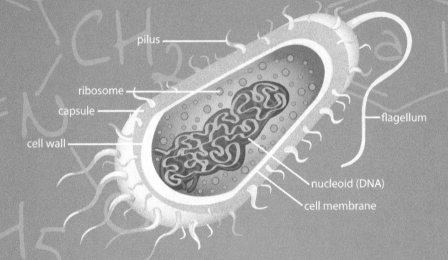

pilus

ribosome

capsule

cell wall

flagellum

nucleoid (DNA)

cell membrane

Their cells don't have a nucleus "command center" that tells the cell what to do. Unlike the cells of plants and animals, their cells don't have lots of organelles that take care of specific functions. The cell walls of their cells are similar to plant cells.

Animal Cell

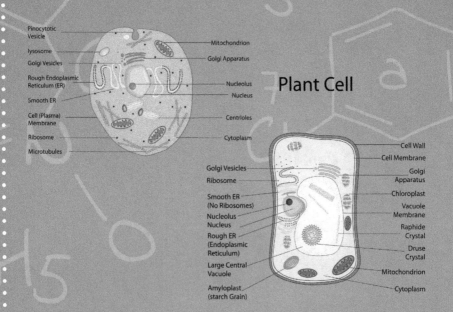

Pinocytotic Vesicle
lysosome
Golgi Vesicles
Rough Endoplasmic Reticulum (ER)
Smooth ER
Cell (Plasma) Membrane
Ribosome
Microtubules

Mitochondrion
Golgi Apparatus
Nucleolus
Nucleus
Centrioles
Cytoplasm

Plant Cell

Golgi Vesicles
Ribosome
Smooth ER (No Ribosomes)
Nucleolus
Nucleus
Rough ER (Endoplasmic Reticulum)
Large Central Vacuole
Amyloplast (starch Grain)

Cell Wall
Cell Membrane
Golgi Apparatus
Chloroplast
Vacuole Membrane
Raphide Crystal
Druse Crystal
Mitochondrion
Cytoplasm

If you study them under a microscope, you'll quickly see that they are all different shapes. Some are rods. Some look like spirals or spheres. Some have long, whip-like structures called flagella that help them move from place to place.

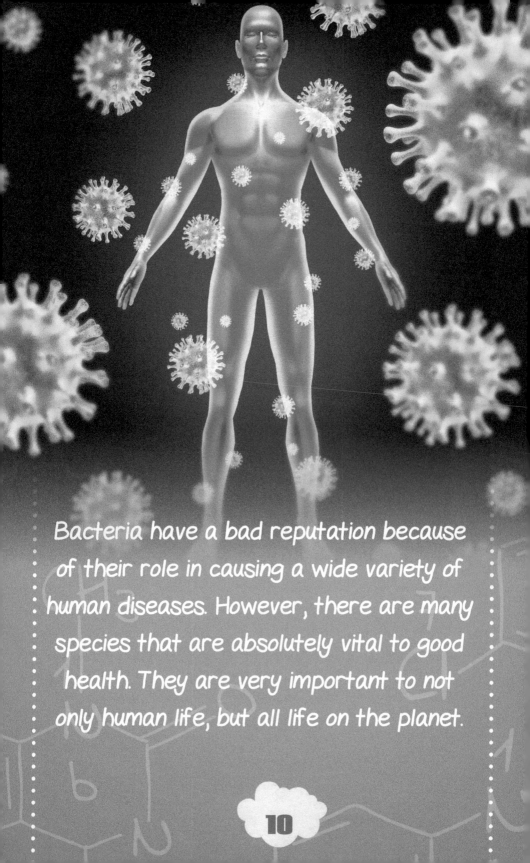

Bacteria have a bad reputation because of their role in causing a wide variety of human diseases. However, there are many species that are absolutely vital to good health. They are very important to not only human life, but all life on the planet.

For example, one species of bacteria that lives in our bodies manufactures vitamin K inside our large intestines, which is a vital factor in blood clotting.

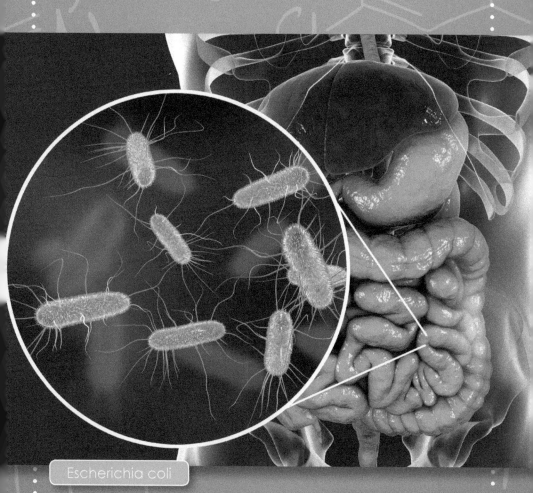

Escherichia coli

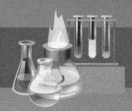

Yogurt

Sourdough Bread

Peas and Soybeans

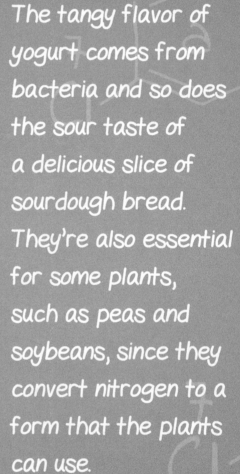

The tangy flavor of yogurt comes from bacteria and so does the sour taste of a delicious slice of sourdough bread. They're also essential for some plants, such as peas and soybeans, since they convert nitrogen to a form that the plants can use.

Who Discovered Bacteria?

Antony Leeuwenhoek

Antony Leeuwenhoek was the first scientist to ever see bacteria and other single-celled organisms through a microscope.

In the late 1670s, he sent detailed drawings of the bacteria and algae he had observed under the microscope to the Royal Society of London. At first they did not believe his findings but then they confirmed his results and the science of microbiology was born.

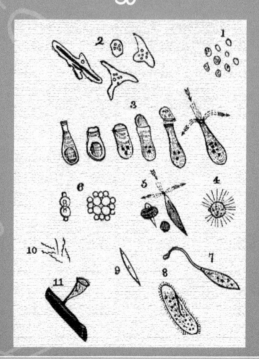

Drawings of the Bacteria and Algae

Scientists have determined that bacteria have been on Earth since 3.5 billion years ago. They are one of the oldest living organisms on Earth.

Archaea, also called archaebacteria, are microscopic prokaryotic organisms that live in incredibly extreme conditions, such as vents from volcanoes and pools that are intensely salty.

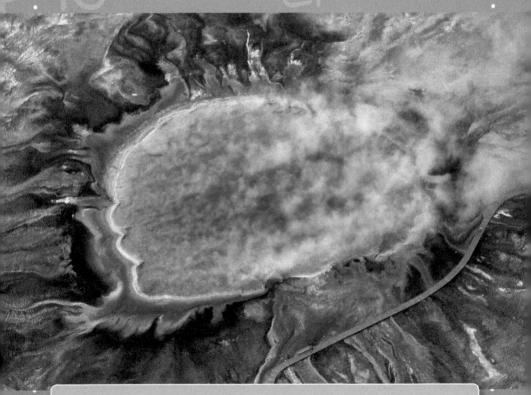

Archaea were found in volcanic hot springs. Pictured here is Grand Prismatic Spring of Yellowstone National Park.

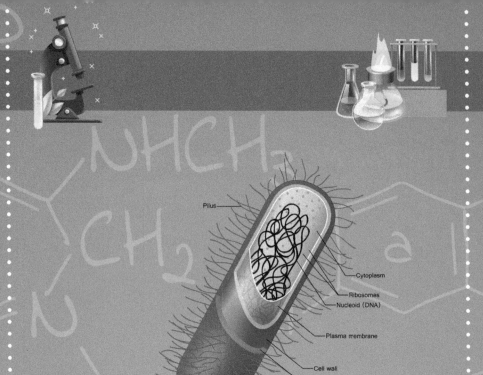

Pilus

Cytoplasm

Ribosomes

Nucleoid (DNA)

Plasma membrane

Cell wall

Capsule

Flagellum

Prokaryotic

Microbiologists believe that bacteria and archaea came from a common ancestor almost four billion years ago. Although they look like bacteria, the archaea are just as different from bacteria as bacteria are different when compared to humans!

The Two Major Categories

There are two major categories of bacteria These categories are autotrophic and heterotrophic.

1. If a bacteria creates its own food through oxidation, then it's called autotrophic.

Autotrophic Bacteria

2.   If a bacteria gets its food from plants or other microorganisms, then it's called heterotrophic.

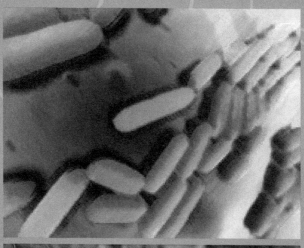

Heterotrophic Bacteria

Another way to group bacteria is by their reaction to oxygen. Aerobic bacteria must have oxygen to survive and will die without it. Anerobic are the opposite. They can't tolerate oxygen and will perish if they're exposed to it.

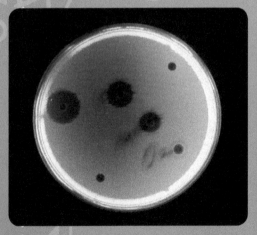

Aerobic Bacteria

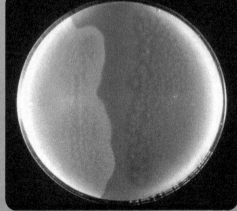

Anerobic Bacteria

The third type called facultative aneraobes would rather have oxygen, but they can live without it.

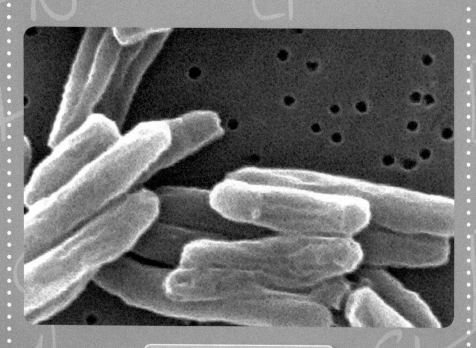

Facultative anaerobe

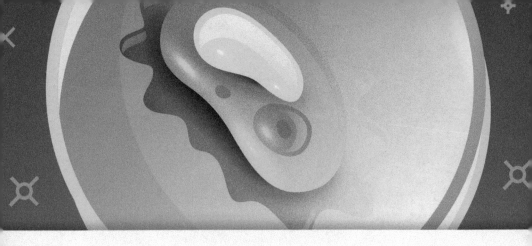

Chapter 2:
Where Can You Find Bacteria?

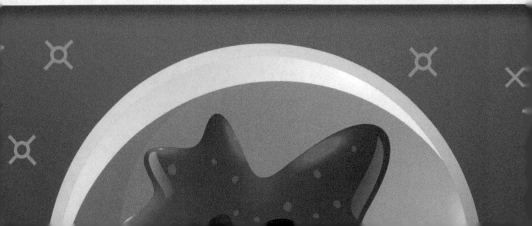

BACTERIA IN THE SOIL

Bacteria and another closely related group called Archaea are the smallest organisms that live in Earth's soil other than viruses. There are more bacteria in the soil than any other type of microorganism.

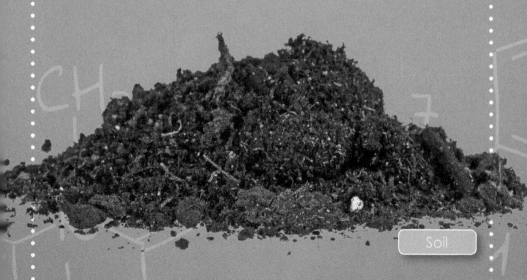

Soil

Bacteria are crucial to the process of decomposition on Earth. They break down organic dead material from both plants and animals and return it in a form that makes the soil rich and fertile. There are more heterotrophic bacteria in the soil than autotrophic, but only the autotrophic bacteria play this vital role in decomposition.

Decomposition of Animal on Green Field

Scientists estimate that there may be as many as 40 million individual bacteria cells in just one gram of soil!

Scientist Studying a soil

BACTERIA IN OUR FOOD

There is a lot of bacteria in our food and in our water. That's why it's important to cook food properly.

For example, E. coli can live in ground meat, but if the meat is cooked to the appropriate temperature it perishes and can't hurt us when we eat the hamburger made out of it.

E. Coli

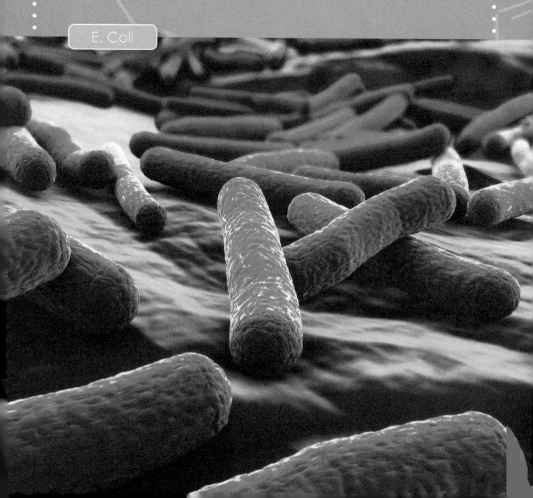

Our water is tested for pathogens that can harm us.

BACTERIA IN OUR BODIES

When we leave our mother's womb, we don't have a single microbe. As we start to travel through the birth canal, whole colonies of bacteria enter our bodies.

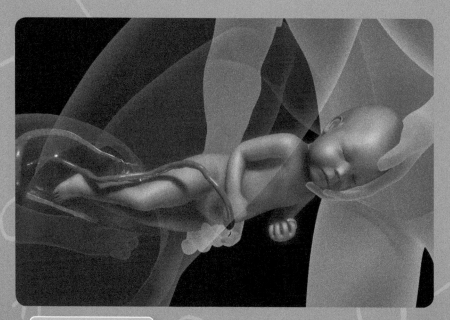

Vaginal Birth

By the time we can crawl, we have come into contact with as many as a hundred trillion microorganisms. They live in our throats, on our skin, and in our intestines.

In fact, over ten thousand species of bacteria live in our bodies and if you put them all together they would weigh as much as our brains. Scientists have coined a term for the bacteria that live on us and in us. They call it our "microbiome." Most of these bacteria are beneficial to us. Scientists are still learning how our bodies interact with bacteria.

Are Bacteria Dangerous?

Most of the bacteria we come into contact with aren't dangerous, but there are some that are and they can make us very sick. The types of bacteria that make us sick are called pathogens. Diseases caused by pathogens affect both animals and plants.

Pathogen Bacteria and Viruses

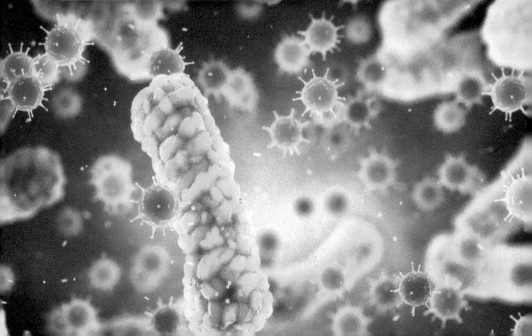

In order to fight off pathogens that create disease, there are some things you can do:

- Wash your hands well and use an antibiotic soap.
- Eat plenty of healthy foods like fruits and vegetables.
- Avoid close contact with people who are coughing, sneezing, and sick.
- Keep any wounds free from harmful bacteria by using antiseptic.
- Take antibiotics as described by your doctor for bacterial diseases and don't overuse them.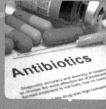

Unfortunately, over time, many types of pathogens develop a resistance to the antibiotics we take to try and fight them.

One of these pathogens that you may have heard of is Escherichia coli called E.coli for short. Most E.coli is harmless and lives well in the human digestive tract. However, some strains of this pathogen can cause very severe food poisoning as well as infections and meningitis, a serious inflammation of the brain.

Food Poisoning

Infections

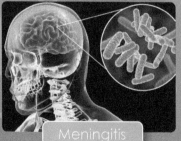
Meningitis

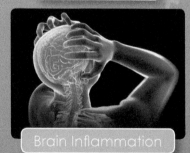
Brain Inflammation

The bacteria that cause tuberculosis, called mycobacterium tuberculosis, have also become resistant to antibiotics over the last twenty years.

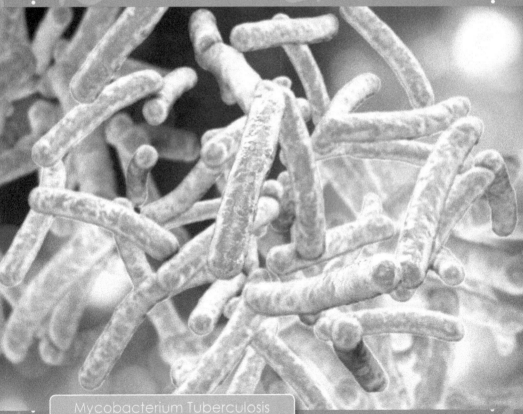

Mycobacterium Tuberculosis

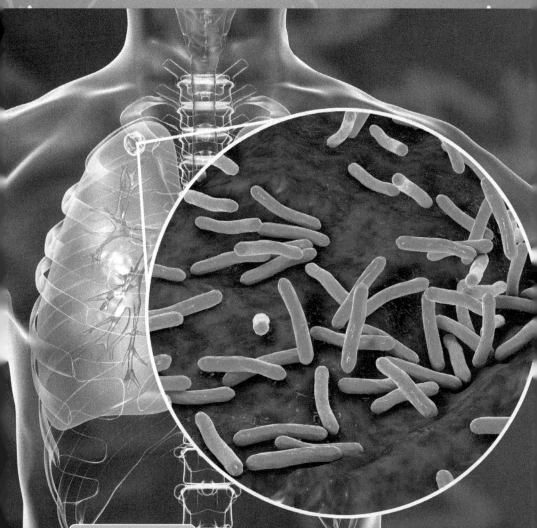

Tuberculosis

Tuberculosis has caused many deaths throughout history and has been found in the remains of bodies 9,000 years old. Documents from ancient Egypt discuss the dangers of the disease and Nefertiti and her husband, the Pharaoh Akhenaten both died from it around 1300 BC.

Nefertiti and her husband, the Pharaoh Akhenaten

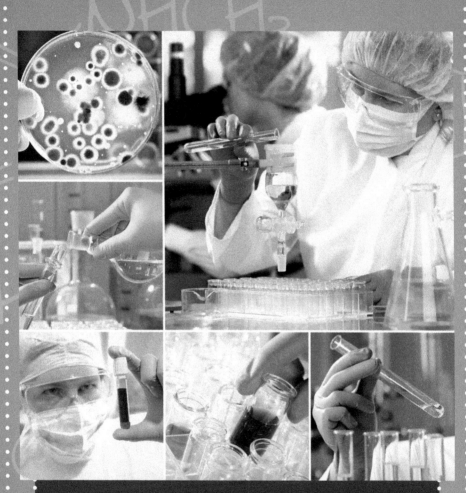

Doctors and scientists are looking for new ways to fight bacteria that are resistant to antibiotics.

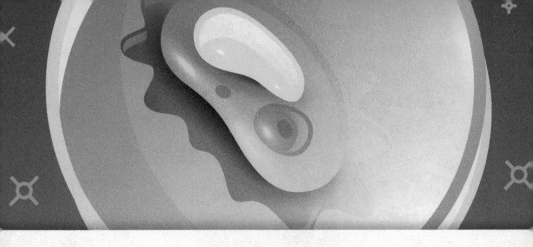

Chapter 3:
What are Protists?

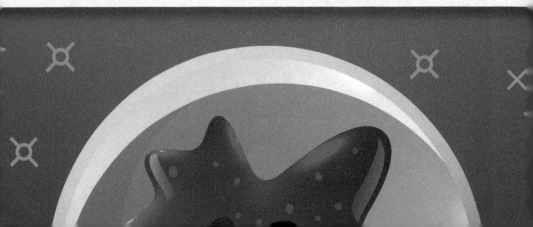

Unlike bacteria, which have very simple cells, protists have eukaryotic cells. This simply means that their cells have a "command center" called the nucleus and other organelles in their cells.

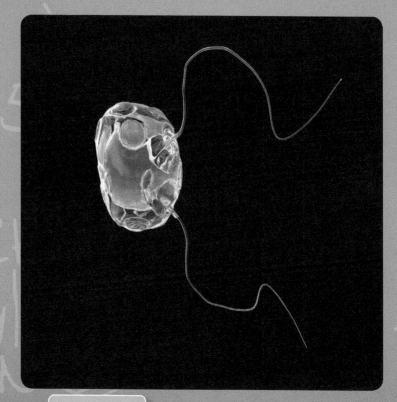

Protists

Most protists are unicellular, but not all of them are. Protists are not animals. They're not plants or fungi either. They fall into a category all their own. In fact, you can think of them as all the eukaryotic organisms that do NOT fall into the category of animals, plants, or fungi.

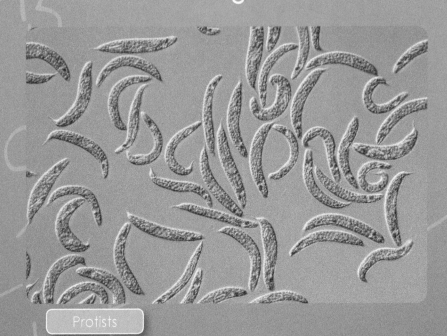

Protists

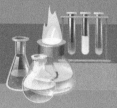

Protozoa, algae, and slime molds fall into the category of protists.

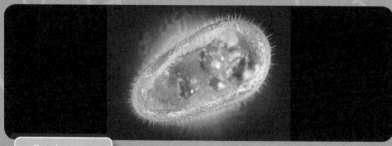

Protozoa

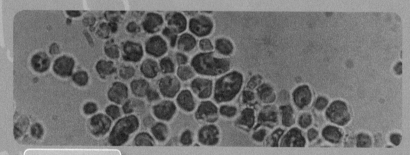

Algae

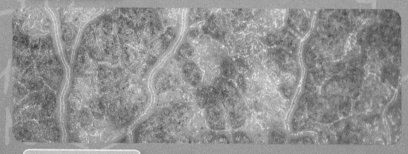

Slime Molds

The Kingdom Protista

Ernst Haeckel

In 1866, when the German biologist Ernst Haeckel first proposed the Kingdom Protista, it wasn't accepted. In fact, it wasn't accepted as a classification until the 1960s.

Slime Mold, Amoeba, Euglena

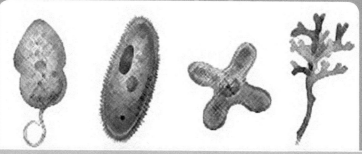

Dinoflagellate, Paramecium, Diatom, Macroalga

The reason is that the organisms in this kingdom are so diverse from each other. In some cases, all they have in common is that they are NOT plants, animals, or fungi. It's been nicknamed the "junk drawer" kingdom for that reason.

Most organisms in the Kingdom Protista are so tiny that they can only be seen using a microscope.

Kingdom Protista

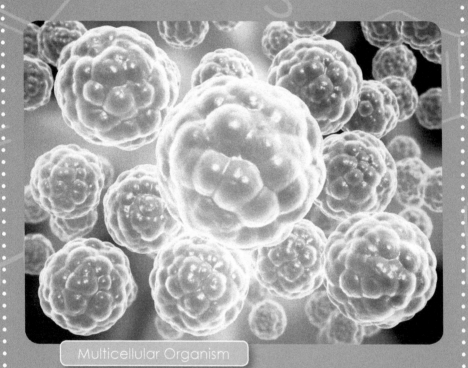

Multicellular Organism

There are a few that are multicellular, which simply means that they have many cells. The multicellular protists can get rather large.

Giant kelp grows in a thick underwater forest

Kelp is a good example of a multicellular protist. If you've ever seen a big piece or pieces of kelp that have washed up on the beach you know how big it can get. Some of them grow to over 100 meters in length. The cells in kelp all look the same. They are eukaryotic cells but they don't differ in function from each other like the cells in your body do.

If you were drawing a diagram and you had bacteria on one side because it has simple cells, and animals and plants on the other because their cells are complex and specialized, protists would fall right in the middle. They have cells that each contain a nucleus, but most of them don't have cells that have specialized tasks.

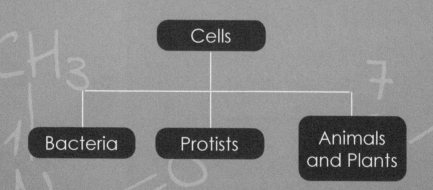

What are the Characteristics of Protists?

There are a few common characteristics of protists.

- They have eukaryotic cells, which means that each of their cells has a nucleus.

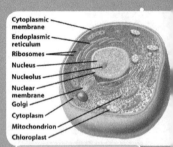

Cytoplasmic membrane
Endoplasmic reticulum
Ribosomes
Nucleus
Nucleolus
Nuclear membrane
Golgi
Cytoplasm
Mitochondrion
Chloroplast

Eukaryotic Cell

- Most of them have mitochondria. These organelles absorb nutrients and transform them into energy for the cell.

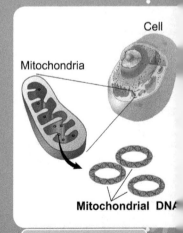

Cell

Mitochondria

Mitochondrial DNA

Mirochondria

- Protists are sometimes parasites. The organism that causes malaria is a protist.

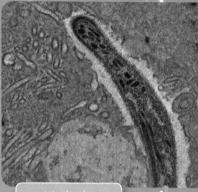

Malaria

- They prefer aquatic environments, but many species can be found in moist soil.

Moist Soil

The protists are a huge category of organisms and scientists are still actively organizing them. They are divided into three main groups based on how similar they are to the animal, plant, and fungi kingdoms.

Protists

What are the Classifications of Protists?

One way that protists can be categorized is by how similar they are to animals, plants, or fungi.

- Animal-like protists, which have the ability to move and must eat other organisms for food
- Plant-like protists, which can create their own food through photosynthesis
- Fungi-like protists, which reproduce by using spores and can't create their own food

Aniaml-like Protists

Plant-like Protists

Fungi-like Protists

There are thousands of species that fall into the Kingdom Protista. These are major categories of the organisms that are generally classified there.

What are the Three Large Categories of Protists?

- Protozoa, which are animal-like protists
- Algae, which are plant-like protists
- Slime Molds, which are fungi-like protists

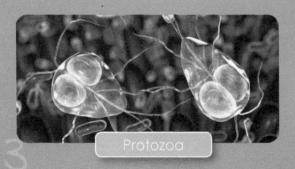
Protozoa

Algae

Slime Molds

How Do Protists Move?

Another way that biologists categorize protists is by the way they move. Different types of protozoa use these three different methods of moving.

- Flagella: These are long, whip-like appendages. Some protozoa have several and some only have one. These flagella help the organism move back and forth.

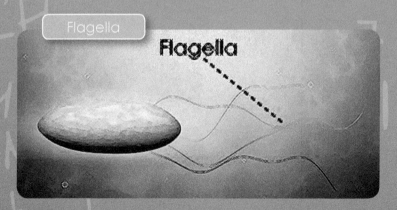

Flagella

- Pseudopodia: An amoeba is one of the types of protists that uses this method. It oozes its body out like a "false foot" to move in a specific direction on a surface.

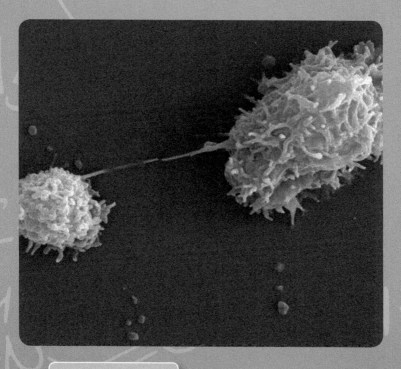

Pseudopodia

● Cilia: Some protozoa use tiny hair-like structures called cilia to move. The cilia move in a wave-like pattern to help the organism move backward and forward.

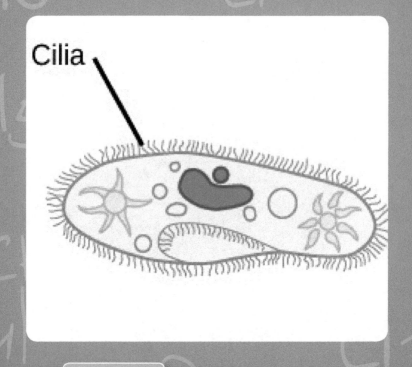

Cilia

Cilia

Do Protists Cause Diseases?

Unfortunately, protists are responsible for some serious human diseases.
In East Africa, a person who is bitten by the Tsetse Fly may get the dreaded Sleeping Sickness. The Tsetse Fly carries the Trypanosoma brucei protozoa and when it bites the person it transfers this deadly parasite.

Tsetse Fly

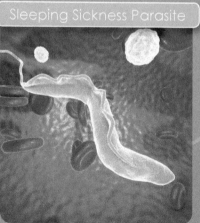

Sleeping Sickness Parasite

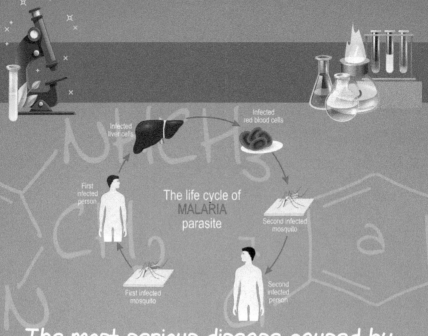

The life cycle of MALARIA parasite

Infected liver cells

Infected red blood cells

First infected person

Second infected mosquito

First infected mosquito

Second infected person

The most serious disease caused by protozoa is malaria. It's caused by Plasmodium. They are parasites of humans as well as mosquitoes. Malaria kills over one million people annually, many of them are children in Africa.

Plasmodium causing Malaria illness

Mosquito Net

Spraying insect repellent on skin

Using a simple mosquito net and preventing mosquito bites from happening is one of the best ways to avoid this deadly disease. There are also antimalarial tablets that people who travel to affected areas can take.

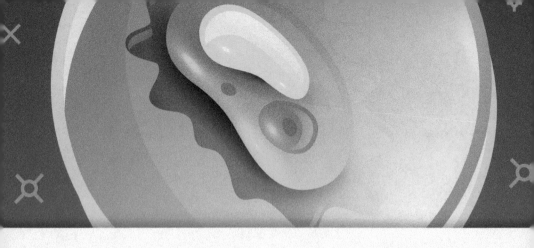

Chapter 4:
Defining Protozoa

Protozoa can be single-celled or multi-celled. Like animals, they track down their food in the environment they are swimming in or moving in. They can be found in freshwater, such as ponds and rivers, marine habitats, and in the soil. They are microscopic.

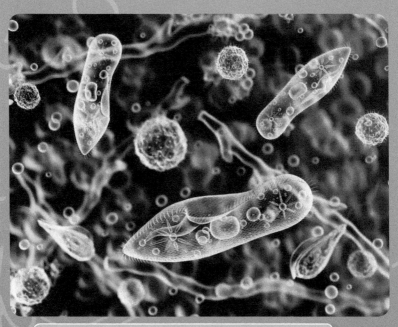

Protozoa, infusoria under a microscope

There are so many different species of protozoa. They are very diverse, which means that they differ in how they move, what they eat, their shape, and their size.

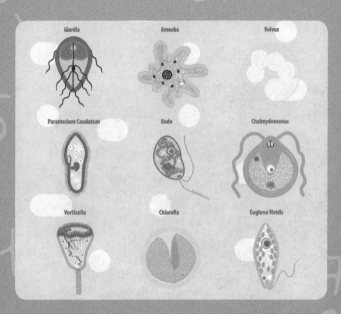

Giardia · Amoeba · Volvox
Paramecium Caudatum · Bodo · Chalmydomonas
Vorticella · Chlorella · Euglena Viridis

Biologists classify them into four different groups: the amoebas, the sporozoans, the ciliates, and the flagellates.

Amoebas produce long extensions of their bodies called pseudopods. When they find a particle of food they want they surround the food with their pseudopod and then they absorb it. Next, they digest it by using special enzymes that break down the food. Another interesting fact about amoebas is that if you divide one in half, the half with the nucleus lives but the other half dies.

Amoeba

The forms of pseudopodia

Sporozoans don't have a way to move by themselves since they don't have flagella, cilia, or pseudopodia. They must live inside a human or animal host as a parasite. These organisms cause disease.

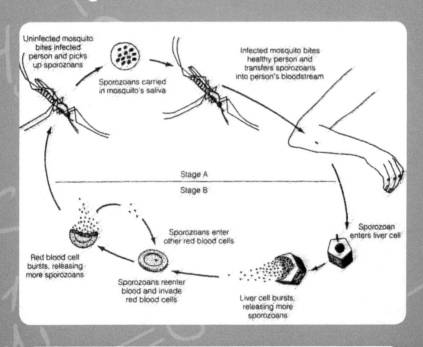

Uninfected mosquito bites infected person and picks up sporozoans

Sporozoans carried in mosquito's saliva

Infected mosquito bites healthy person and transfers sporozoans into person's bloodstream

Stage A

Stage B

Sporozoan enters liver cell

Red blood cell bursts, releasing more sporozoans

Sporozoans enter other red blood cells

Sporozoans reenter blood and invade red blood cells

Liver cell bursts, releasing more sporozoans

Sporozoans living inside a human and animal host

A paramecium is an example of a ciliate. As its cilia move back and forth, they cause the paramecium to move forward while it is spinning.

Paramecium

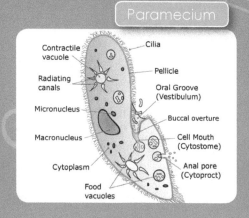

A Trypanosoma brucei is an example of a protozoan flagellate. It uses its whip-like flagella to move.

Trypanosoma Brucei

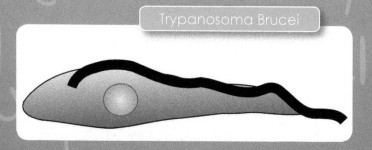

Some protozoa that live under the sea create shells to live in and when the organisms die these go to the bottom of the sea. Even though they're very small, there have been so many over 600 million years that today's chalk and limestone rocks are made up primarily of those shells!

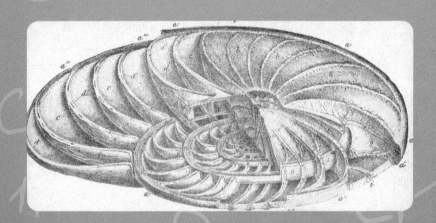

Lime Shell

What is an Algae?

Algae are sometimes categorized to be part of the plant kingdom and sometimes they are considered to be protists. According to some recent studies of evolutionary relationships, red algae and also green algae are most closely connected to plants. However, there are other types of algae that seem to be more closely related to certain groups within the protists.

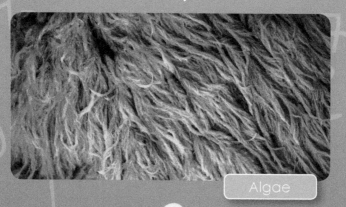

Algae

New algae are discovered all the time, and as scientists learn more about them classifications may change. The scientists who feel that algae aren't plants argue that plants have specialized tissues, such as stems, roots, and leaves, so they feel that algae belong in the "junk drawer" of protists.

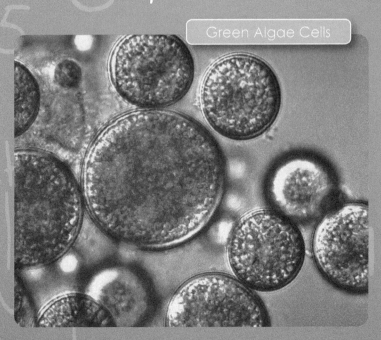

Green Algae Cells

One thing is certain. If you classify algae as a protist, then it is definitely a plant-like protist since it makes its own food through photosynthesis. Algae contain chlorophyll, which is a green pigment that absorbs light to give the energy for photosynthesis. In other words, it's solar power in its most natural form. The many different types of algae are sometimes organized by their colors of green, brown, yellow, and red.

Green, Brown, Yellow and Red Algae

Nearly 50 percent of the photosynthesis on Earth is done by algae, so whether you consider them a plant or a protist, algae are critical to the environment.

Green algae grow on the surface of the lake

What are Slime Molds?

Slime molds are not the same types of molds that fall into the fungi category. The slime molds that are protists fall into two categories: cellular slime molds and plasmodial slime molds.

Cellular Slime Molds

Plasmodial Slime Molds

Cellular slime molds are small and unicellular, which means they have one cell. However, to make the mold they work together as if they were a single organism. Different types of unicellular slime molds will work at different tasks when they join together as one organism. This is a simpler way of having specialized cells than the specialization that animals or humans have in their bodies.

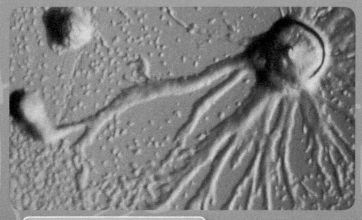

Cellular Slime Molds

Plasmodial slime molds are the opposite of cellular slime molds. They are just made from one cell. Even though they're only one cell they can get several feet in width. They can have more than one nucleus as a "command center" in their one cell as well.

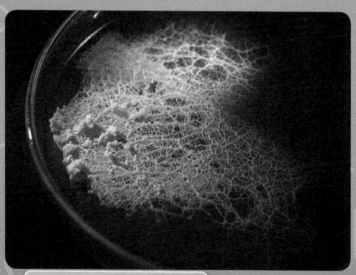

Plasmodial Slime Molds

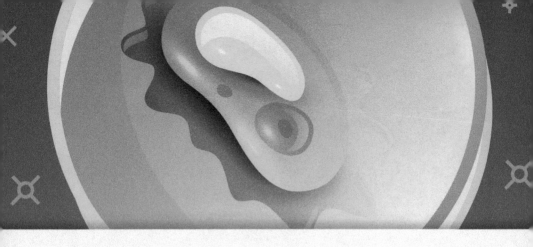

Chapter 5:
What Are Fungi?

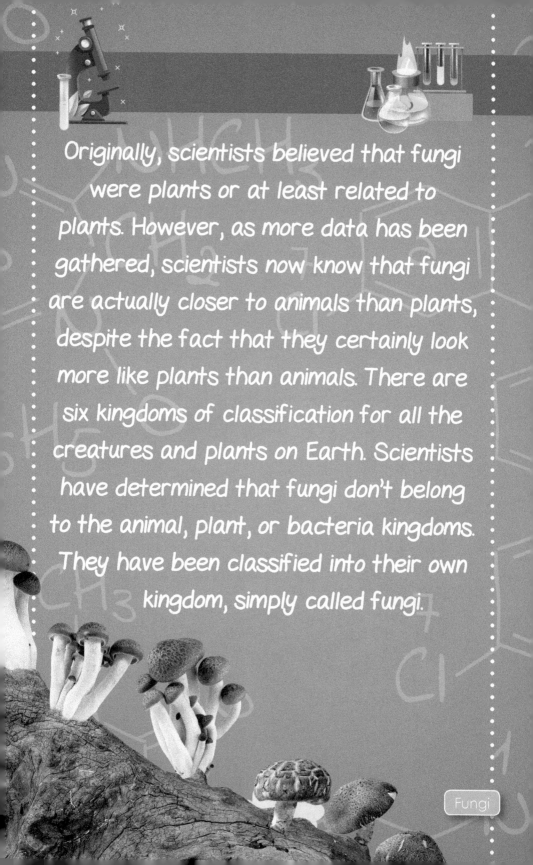

Originally, scientists believed that fungi were plants or at least related to plants. However, as more data has been gathered, scientists now know that fungi are actually closer to animals than plants, despite the fact that they certainly look more like plants than animals. There are six kingdoms of classification for all the creatures and plants on Earth. Scientists have determined that fungi don't belong to the animal, plant, or bacteria kingdoms. They have been classified into their own kingdom, simply called fungi.

Fungi

Fungi's Two Main Cell Categories

One of the clues that molds and other type of fungi are not related to bacteria has to do with their cell structure.

There are lots of different types of cells that make up plants and animals but they fall into two main categories.

Fungus

A simple cell that doesn't have a nucleus to instruct it what to do is called a prokaryotic cell. Bacteria have these types of cells.

The other main type of cell is a lot larger and quite a bit more complicated than a prokaryotic cell. It's called a eukaryote cell and it has lots of different parts compared to the elementary type of prokaryotic cell.

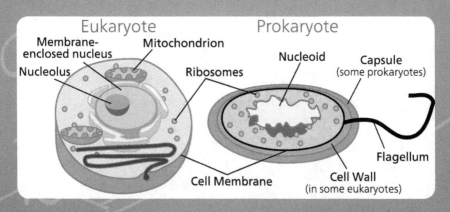

Eukaryote   Prokaryote

Membrane-enclosed nucleus   Mitochondrion   Nucleoid   Capsule (some prokaryotes)

Nucleolus   Ribosomes

Cell Membrane   Cell Wall (in some eukaryotes)   Flagellum

What are the Characteristics of Fungi?

If you were a scientist trying to identify whether a sample could be classified as a fungus, you would consider the following characteristics.

- Fungi have eukaryotic cells instead of prokaryotic cells.

- Fungi get their food one of two ways. They consume decomposing matter or they are parasites and eat the bodies of their hosts, which can be either plants or animals.

Fungi Autumn Mushroon

- They don't have any chlorophyll cells and that means they don't make their own food by photosynthesis.

- They don't reproduce using pollen, seeds, or fruit like plants do. Instead, they reproduce through a large amount of spores.

- Similar to plants, they can't usually move by their own power.

Orange Pore fungus

Are They Plants?

Fungi

Fungi have eukaryote cells like animals and plants do instead of the prokaryotic cells that bacteria have. Because of that, they're not related to bacteria. Even though their cell structure is similar to plants they're not plants because they differ from plants in two very important ways.

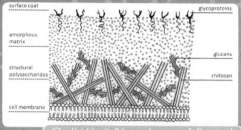
Cell Wall Structure of Fungi

The cells walls of fungi are made of chitin while the cell walls of plants are made of cellulose. Chitin is a type of fibrous substance that forms the exoskeletons of certain

Exoskeleton of Crab

animals. For example, the exoskeleton of a crab is made of chitin. In this way, fungi more closely resemble animals than plants.

The other major difference is that unlike plants they don't make their own food. Plants make their own food using a process called photosynthesis.

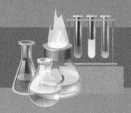

For a long time, scientists classified fungi with the lower plants. These were plants such as mosses, ferns, and also liverworts. Fungi have been classified in their own kingdom since 1969. Recently, scientists have compared their DNA sequences as well as their cell structure to plants and animals.

Moss, Fern and Liverworts

Even though fungi in some cases grow out of the ground and don't move, they're actually more similar to animals than plants. So, when you see a mushroom growing in your backyard, remember it's a type of fungus, not a plant!

Mushroom growing in the backyard

Why Are They Important?

Fungi are very important in the world's food chain. We wouldn't have many types of bread products without the use of yeast. Yeast is a very simple type of fungi that are round and single celled.

Dry Yeast

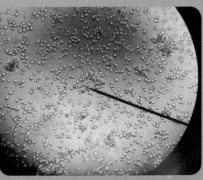

Yeast Cells Under the Microscope

There are also many different types of edible mushrooms that both animals and humans eat. Fungi also play a very important part in decomposition. They break down dead organic matter and while they are using that matter for their own nutrients, they release carbon, oxygen, and nitrogen into the soil and the air.

The fungi on this tree are decomposers

Some types of fungi are very important in medicines used to heal people. Antibiotics that kill bacterial infections, such as penicillin, are made from fungi.

Medicinal Mushrooms, Lingzhi Mushroom

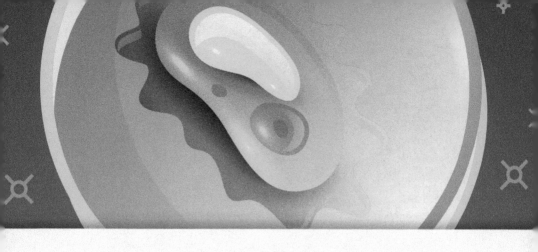

Chapter 6:
Other Types of Microorganisms

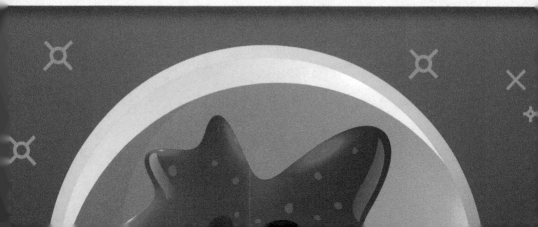

The microorganisms in our soil are very important because they affect the structure of the soil as well as its fertility. Fertile soil yields more food for animals and people and helps plants grow. Each group of microorganisms has a specific function in the soil.

Soil Microorganism

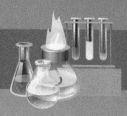

Other than those already mentioned, below are other types of microorganisms:

ACTINOMYCETES

Actinomycetes are a type of bacteria but they fall in a separate category because they

Actinomycetes

have similar characteristics to fungi. Their shapes as well as their branching properties are like those of fungi. They form long filaments that stretch through soil. They also decompose material in a similar way as fungi. However, like bacteria, their cells don't have a defined nucleus.

Actinomycetes have three very important functions.

- They provide us with many important antibiotics used in medicine.
- They fix nitrogen, which means they convert nitrogen from the air so plants can use it.
- They decompose tough materials, such as plant tissues, such as paper, stems from plants, and bark from trees. They can even decompose the hard exoskeletons of insects!

Actinomycete Webbing On Tree Stump

Scientists discovered that actinomycetes somehow kept the populations of bacterial in soil in balance. This led two scientists, named Selman Waksman and Albert Shatz to think that these microorganisms could be used to fight diseases caused by bacteria, such as tuberculosis. Their research led to lots of medicines used to fight bacterial diseases.

Selamn Waksman

Albert Shatz

Actinomycetes are responsible for two-thirds of the antibiotics we use today. Here are a few examples of these healing antibiotics:

- Streptomycin, used to treat tuberculosis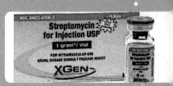
- Neomycin, used to reduce bacterial infection during surgery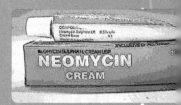
- Erythromycin, used to treat bronchitis and pneumonia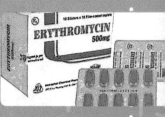
- v, used to heal urinary tract infections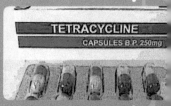

NEMATODES

Nematodes are worms that are not segmented. They are about 1/20 of an inch long and 1/500 of an inch in diameter. There are a few nematodes that are responsible for plant diseases but most nematodes are beneficial.

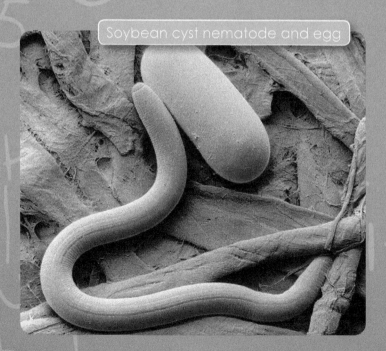

Soybean cyst nematode and egg

Nematodes are very important to the food web of the soil. Some eat plants and algae. Some eat fungi and bacteria and some eat other nematodes. Like protozoa they release nutrients in forms that plants can use.

Nematode in Soil

Chapter 7:

What Is An Epidemic?

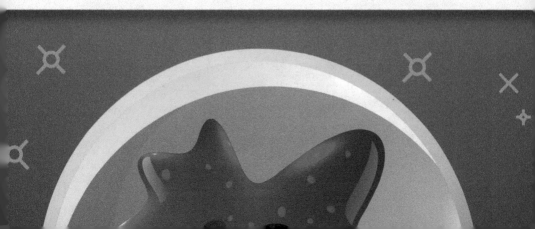

When a very large population gets sick at the same time with an infectious disease, it's called an epidemic. For example, in 1867, over 3,000 people in New Orleans died from contracting yellow fever.

Children in St. Vincent's Asylum, New Orleans, Attended by Sisters of Charity

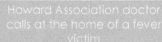

Howard Association doctor calls at the home of a fever victim

Bodies were quickly buried in mass graves at Elmwood and other cemeteries.

An epidemic can be started in numerous ways. Lack of sanitary conditions is one of the major causes, but there are other reasons as well.

- Wars and Natural Disasters
- Introduction of a Disease into a Geographic Area
- Lower Immunity to a Disease
- Infected Sources of Food or Water
- A Disease Becomes More Virulent

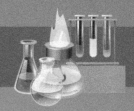

How Do Diseases Spread?

Disease can be spread in a number of different ways. Unsanitary conditions that cause food or drinking water to be unsafe can cause diseases to spread. Examples of diseases that are transmitted this way are:

- Cholera, which causes watery diarrhea and severe vomiting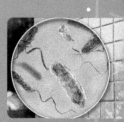
- Dysentery, which causes bloody diarrhea
- Typhoid Fever, which causes severe headaches, stomach pain, and loss of appetite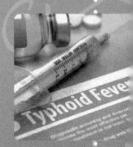

Another way that disease spreads is through the air. For example, if you have the flu and you cough or sneeze, you can spread the infection to another person. In addition to influenza, which is also called the flu, two other types of diseases that are transmitted in the air are tuberculosis and measles.

Spreading Infection

Tuberculosis

Measles

Insects frequently carry different types of diseases and can transmit them to large populations of people. For example, mosquitoes can carry malaria and fleas can carry bubonic plague.

MALARIA TRANSMISSION CYCLE

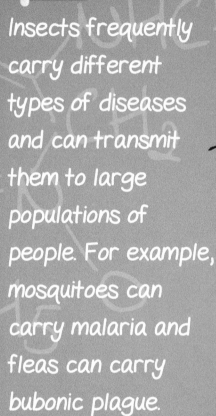

Yersinia pestis

Xenopsylla cheopis

BUBONIC PLAGUE

How Do Epidemics End?

Epidemics spread rapidly and can kill millions of people. At some point, they do stop, at least for a while, until another outbreak occurs. There are quite a few reasons why an epidemic stops.

One reason is that there are fewer carriers of the disease. For example, certain types of mosquitoes carry malaria. During the cold weather, there are less mosquitoes to transmit the disease, so this may slow down or stop the cases of malaria.

Some types of diseases happen more often during certain times of the year. For example, epidemics of the flu happen in the winter more often than at other times of the year. One reason is that the flu virus survives better in moist air.

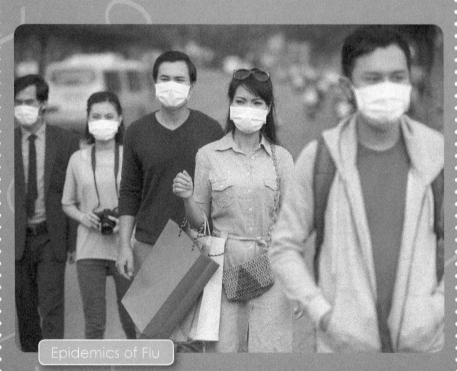

Epidemics of Flu

Another reason that epidemics eventually die out is because they can't find appropriate hosts. When a disease first strikes, it attacks the weakest people. Babies, elderly people, and adults with weakened immune systems are usually the first to become infected. However, if these people fight off the disease they can build up immunity to it. Over time, the disease finds less and less hosts who are easy to infect.

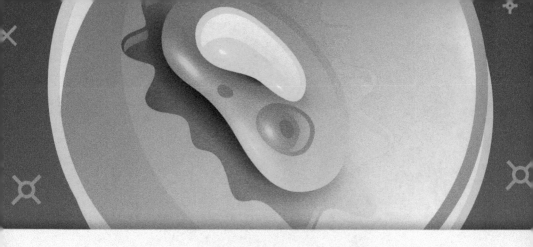

Chapter 8:
What Are Pandemics?

A pandemic is defined as an epidemic that has infected a large geographic region, such as more than one country, more than one continent, or across the world.

There are six specific stages of an epidemic that's become a pandemic. These stages have been defined by the World Health Organization, which is a special United Nations agency whose mission is the health of people worldwide.

Stage 1: The virus is detected in animals. It hasn't been transmitted to humans yet.

Stage 2: The virus infects humans.

Stage 3: There are outbreaks of the disease, but it isn't spreading quickly.

Stage 4: There are human-to-human transmissions of the disease. Whole communities are now infected and the disease has caused an epidemic.

Stage 5: The virus has spread through one country and is threatening a second country. The disease is moving rapidly and a full-scale pandemic is likely to happen.

Stage 6: The epidemic is now a full-scale pandemic.

THE WORST EPIDEMICS AND PANDEMICS IN HISTORY

There have been many epidemics throughout history and some increased to the size that they were pandemics. Each of them had a huge impact on human history.

The Plague of Athens in 430 BC to 427 BC

This plague began while the city-state of Athens was fighting against the city-state of Sparta. The disease, which most scholars believe was typhoid fever, lingered for over three years. About one fourth of the people living in Athens died including their leader Pericles. Because of the heavy toll of the plague, Athens lost the war against Sparta.

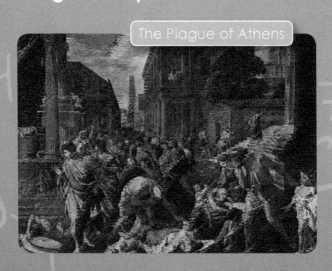

The Plague of Athens

The Plague of Justinian in 541 to 542 AD

This plague was one of the first occurrences of the dreaded bubonic plague. It expanded throughout Eastern Europe. At the time, the Emperor Justinian ruled this empire, which was called the Byzantine Empire. During the worst part of the plague, about 5,000 people were dying daily in the city of Constantinople. Even the emperor himself became ill, but he was able to survive. For the next two centuries, the bubonic plague came back many times. The historical impact of the disease was that the Byzantium Empire couldn't continue its expansion.

The Plague of Justinian

The Black Death from 1347 to 1350 AD

The Black Death pandemic spread through Europe rapidly during the Middle Ages. There wasn't a cure and once it got into people's lungs it was very contagious, which simply means that it transmitted very fast from person to person. At that time, scientists and physicians had no clue how the disease had started. Today

it's believed that unsanitary conditions in Asia caused the disease. Black rats were infected to start, then, fleas bit them and became infected. The fleas bit humans who subsequently also became infected. However, recent evidence points to gerbils instead of rats as the initial cause of the disease. More than likely, the plague got to Europe from Asia on merchant ships manned by Europeans.

The Black Death

It's difficult to imagine how frightening the Black Death was. In Paris, more than 800 people were dying every day. There were so many people dying at the same time that their bodies had to be brought to massive pits to be buried.

The citizens of Tournai, Belgium, burying the dead during the Black Death

Conditions were very unsanitary during the Middle Ages so there were rats and fleas everywhere. The fleas continued to infect people and once someone got the disease into his lungs he developed a pneumonia form of the disease. Then it was transmitted person to person by coughing and sneezing. The disease caused black- and blue-colored blotches over the skin of its victims as they coughed up blood. In Europe and Asia, between 75 million to 200 million people were wiped out by the Black Death. Over 20 million people died in Europe alone, which was over one third of the total population. Today, there are still cases of bubonic plague, but it can be treated with

antibiotics so people who become infected can still survive.

The bubonic plague came back to Europe numerous times. During the bubonic plague of 1656 AD, doctors wore bird-like masks to protect themselves as they tended to patients. The beaks in these masks had strong fragrances to ward off the horrible smells of the infection.

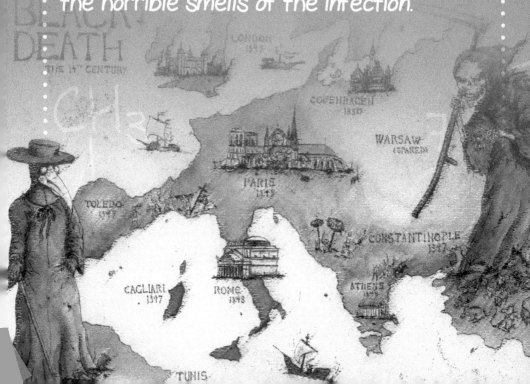

The Spanish Flu from 1918 to 1920 AD

The influenza virus, known as the Spanish flu, started to spread globally very quickly. Eventually, it infected over 500 million. Of those infected, it's estimated that 50 to 100 million of them were killed.

during the influenza pandemic of 1918

This took place during World War I. Since Spain wasn't fighting in the war, they reported news about the flu and the toll it was taking. Other countries in Europe

as well as the United States also had huge outbreaks of the flu, but due to the war they weren't given permission to report on the loss of life in the newspapers.

Microorganisms are either good or evil. They can cause life to flourish on Earth but in some cases, they also cause death. Study more about them by doing your own research.

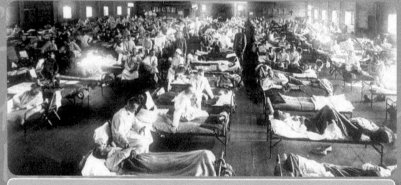

Emergency military hospital during influenza epidemic

Visit

www.SpeedyBookStore.com

To view and download free content on your
favorite subject and browse our catalog of
new and exciting books for readers of all
ages.

Lightning Source UK Ltd.
Milton Keynes UK
UKHW021134130223
416877UK00004B/14